EXPOSED

7 WAYS DEMONS INVADE YOUR LIFE

YOUR 5-STEP GUIDE TO RECOGNIZING & DEFEATING DEMONIC OPPRESSION

DONNA HOWELLS

Exposed: 7 Ways Demons Invade Your Life

Your 5-Step Guide to Recognizing and Defeating Demonic Oppression

Donna Howells

Harrison House

Published by Harrison House Publishers, Shippensburg, PA 17257

ISBN 13 TP: 978-1-6675-1448-2

ISBN 13 eBook: 978-1-6675-1449-9

For Worldwide Distribution, Printed in the U.S.A.

1 2 3 4 5 6 7 8 / 28 27 26 25 24

Contents

Foreword

Donna and her husband Robbie have experienced what real deliverance ministry is all about. This book is undoubtedly an eye-opener that ventures into the deliverance arena armed with a solid biblical foundation and birthed from a place of practice and discernment. The stories and testimonies are raw and straightforward, and the whole journey started because of one quasi-routine phone call.

Since my early years, I have encountered many people with dramatic stories and cases of deliverance, ranging from witches to regular people who dealt with demonic issues. Every demon came out in the name of Jesus. This book, however, deals with deliverance from a place of great sensitivity and honesty. Tough questions such as, "Can a Christian have a demon?" and more issues like it are addressed here—with clarity, I might add. Enlightening points are made by Donna as "deliverance of the saints" is a massive part of her ministry. She shows us that demons impact the souls of humanity, saved and unsaved alike, and knowing how to navigate this issue will be helpful for every reader.

As I read through the pages of this book, I found myself saying, "This is a well-rounded understanding of deliverance," and thought several times that Donna offers a healthy take on this issue. On each page, I found myself thinking about the matters Donna addresses as they are thought-provoking yet straightforward. The reader will find out that demons have personalities. They are wicked and evil spirits, and depending on the type of demon they are, their character traits will take over someone's personality without them even realizing it! You will then find out how to drive those evil spirits out!

Demons cannot stop the call of God on your life, but they can delay it by making it difficult for you to recognize that God has given you everything needed to accomplish what He has called you to do. Demons will do their best to make you content with living your Christian life without vision, victory, or true freedom in Christ. If the devil can't kill you, he will steal from you; if that doesn't work, he will try to destroy you. Maybe he can't take your life, but he will try and make your life a living hell while you're on earth, hoping you will turn away from God by losing all faith and trust in Him.

To combat the demonic influences we are facing at an all-time high, Donna unashamedly deals with real-world issues; she pulls back the cover on the kingdom of darkness and its wicked tactics and sheds light on the open doors by which the demonic attempts to access your life. It was refreshing to read how she skillfully deals with counseling and deliverance by showing that these two areas can work well together. She additionally made every instance she described understandable by conveying with transparency areas where these issues hit close to home.

What I found refreshing and encouraging about this book is the absence of learned religious overtones, but rather a significant level of biblical clarity and raw honesty. Here is a book that will assist anyone wanting to understand deliverance and utilize it as a step-by-step guide for operating in it.

Thank you to Donna for writing such a necessary and clear book on this vital subject! For many years to come, this book will be a source and point of reference on the topic of deliverance. I pray this written work finds itself in the right hands at the right time and that those who read this book find the answers they seek.

Maybe the person I'm praying for is you. God bless you as you read.

Joseph Z

Author, broadcaster, prophetic voice
JosephZ.com

Introduction: The Personalities Behind the Darkness

Demons have personalities. They are not abstract forces or nameless evils floating in the unseen realm—they are intelligent, willful, and cunning spiritual beings with motives, strategies, and distinct characteristics. They talk, think, reason, and manipulate. Their goal is simple yet devastating: to distort the image of God in His people. They know that while they cannot erase your salvation, they can twist your perception of who you are in Christ until you no longer live in the fullness of His calling.

I've watched it happen time and again. A person who loves Jesus—faithful in prayer, generous in heart, sincere in worship—begins to lose joy. Then peace slips away. Then hope fades. Before long, that person no longer walks in victory but in quiet defeat. What happened? Somewhere along the way, they came into agreement with a personality that was not their own.

Jesus warned us plainly in John 10:10: *"The thief does not come except to steal, and to kill, and to destroy."* Many of us love the second half of that verse—*"I have come that they may have life, and have it more abundantly."* Yet if we do not understand the first half, we risk missing why Jesus came in the first place. The abundant life He promised is not automatic—it must be guarded from the thief who is determined to destroy it.

Satan's kingdom operates through deception. He and his demons thrive in darkness—whispering lies until those lies sound like your own thoughts. They tell you that you are worthless, hopeless, too sinful, too broken, too far gone. They remind you of every failure, every wound, every rejection, and they do it with such subtlety that you begin to believe the narrative they feed you. Before long, you are living out the identity they've written for you instead of the one God declared over you.

But here's the truth: those voices are not yours. Every thought that contradicts the Word of God is a foreign voice. When Scripture tells us to *"be transformed by the renewing of your mind"* (Romans 12:2), it's not just good advice—it's a divine command for spiritual warfare. We are not battling flesh and blood, but *"principalities, powers, rulers of the darkness of this age, spiritual hosts of wickedness in the heavenly places"* (Ephesians 6:12).

Deliverance, therefore, is not an event—it's a process of reclaiming what belongs to Christ in you. It begins with honesty, continues with forgiveness, and ends with freedom. You cannot confront what you hide. You cannot cast out what you still embrace. Satan is a legalist—he knows that any sin or unforgiveness left in the dark gives him the right to remain. But when you bring it into the light through confession, repentance, and the power of Jesus' name, his grip is broken.

I've seen the difference desperation makes. Those who come hungry for freedom—like the woman with the issue of blood, pressing through the crowd just to touch the hem of His garment—find it. Not because deliverance ministers are powerful, but because Jesus is. The Holy Spirit shows up where humility and desperation meet.

In the pages that follow, you will learn not only how demons operate, but how to recognize their personalities, expose their lies, and cast them out through the authority of Christ. This is not about fear—it's about victory. God has not left you powerless or vulnerable. You have been given everything you need to walk in free-

dom, but it begins with one essential truth:

You are not your thoughts. You are not your wounds. You are not what the enemy says you are. You are who God says you are—and when you know that, every demon in hell must bow to the name of Jesus.

Chapter 1
Access Granted: How the Enemy Finds His Way In

Demons have personalities. They are wicked and evil spirits, and depending on the type of demon they are, their character traits will take over a person's personality without them even realizing it! Demons cannot stop the call of God on your life, but they can delay it by making it difficult for you to recognize that God has given you everything needed to accomplish what He has called you to do.

Demons will do their best to make you content with living your Christian life without vision, victory, or true freedom in Christ.

While we remember John 10:10 mostly for the second or latter part of the scripture where Jesus declares that He has come to give us life and life more abundantly, the first part of the scripture must be taken seriously and understood. Jesus reminds us that the thief who is Satan comes *only* to kill, steal, and destroy—this is his main objective. If he can't kill you, then he will steal from you, and if that doesn't work, then he will try to destroy you. Maybe he can't take your life, but he will try and make your life a living hell while you're on earth, hoping that you will turn away from God by losing all faith and trust in Him.

Demons will continually make you feel insignificant, not holy enough or good enough. They know pretty much all the Bible, so they will quote scripture to you and use it against you. If you are not aware that demons are on the inside of you and that you are oppressed by them, then you will start to believe *their* thoughts are your thoughts. You will listen unknowingly to what they are saying and start to believe that you are depressed, suicidal, angry, lonely, worried, and full of anxiety. You will start to identify with these traits and believe this is who you are. This is them, not you! The word of God says we have the mind of Christ once we are born again, so every thought that is contrary to God's way of thinking comes from one of two places—our thoughts or a demon's thoughts (masquerading as our thoughts). Satan has the art of suggestion down to a tee; he is a master at this type of attack on the believer, and he uses this strategy repeatedly because it works so well for him. We must not take the thoughts of a demon on, and the way we recognize them is that their thoughts are contrary to what God's word says about us. This is why it says in Romans 12:2 (NKJV) that we are to renew our minds in the word of God:

And do not be conformed to this world, but be transformed by the renewing of your mind, that you may prove what is that good and acceptable and perfect will of God.

Second Corinthians 10:3-6 (NKJV) instructs us to pull down every vain imagination that sets itself up against God's word. In fact, it's one of the clearest scriptures in the

Bible that lets us know who we are fighting against—spiritual beings, principalities, powers, rulers of wickedness in heavenly places!

For though we walk in the flesh, we do not war according to the flesh. For the weapons of our warfare are not carnal but mighty in God for pulling down strongholds, casting down arguments and every high thing that exalts itself against the knowledge of God, bringing every thought into captivity to the obedience of Christ, and being ready to punish all disobedience when your obedience is fulfilled.

Before you start panicking, thinking you are demon-possessed or that you somehow have a demon hanging off the back of you, let me say this—*stop, stay calm,* and carry on! I am going to break it all down for you in the next couple of chapters. Trust me, there will be no gray areas left untouched. You will *know* by the end of this whether you need deliverance (welcome to the club!), and you will understand the significance of the deliverance ministry for the church in these last days. Then, most importantly, you will know how you can personally operate in deliverance, bringing hope and freedom to others.

First, let me explain to you *how* and *when* demons gain entry and then answer the question of exactly *where* they enter in the next chapter.

Trauma of any kind is usually the open door that initially allows a demon to enter. Once they are in, they will wait for opportune moments to start to distort how you think and feel about yourself, and because there is no time frame with them, this could happen straight away or years after you have experienced that initial trauma. Whatever area you have experienced trauma in—sexual, emotional, or physical—is the point where the distortion will start. Demons will do this through your mind and your thought processes, which will then affect your will and emotions, ultimately heading for your heart, as you will read in the next chapter.

As in the case of my associate pastor, it was her past that had opened a door in her life when she was a little girl, illustrating my earlier point that messed up adults are generally a result of messed up childhoods. Every experience in our lives creates good or bad memories that stay with us right through to the day we die. Not all memories are significant or bad, which is why we forget some things, although a song or a smell will remind us of our past as if it happened only yesterday. The problem is the memories that *are* bad—the ones we have fought hard to forget, the ones we have put to the very back of our minds, wishing or pretending they never happened. We know if we think about them, they will take us to a dark place in our minds and even cause our bodies to physically react. The moment we think of them, it's like being transported back in time. We feel bound and restricted with fear, guilt, shame, or terror. It's these types of feelings that allow demons to enter. The trauma attracts them, and our emotions open a spiritual door into our soul (mind, will, and emotions), and whether it's in our past or something we are experiencing now, it's what allows a demon to gain access.

Let me clarify. Demons gain their entry in our lives through traumatic experiences that produce, to name a few, fear, guilt, shame, violence, rejection, abandonment, or terror. These come through sin, which we have committed in our past or present, but also, sadly, often it is through sin that has been committed *against* us. The experiences are as individual as we are, and here are just a few examples of open doors or entry points where demons have come in. Hopefully knowing this will help you gain a clearer understanding of demonic oppression and bring clarity to how demons operate.

Chapter 2
Entrance Through Abuse

T his would be the longest book ever written if I wrote down an account of every person I have delivered as a direct result of abuse. Abuse comes in various forms—physical, sexual, and emotional. It could be any one or all three of these abuses that has happened to you, or you may have been witness to the abuse of a family member or friend, or you could be the perpetrator of the abuse. Whatever category you fit into, demons don't care—they just see an open door and they take their opportunity. Abuse is a violation against us; it doesn't seek permission, it just demands our compliance. Abuse will take something that doesn't belong to it, leaving the abused person feeling robbed and defiled. This is the very nature of a demon; they steal what doesn't belong to them. Demons of abuse will make their hosts feel guilty and shamed for being abused and will try and make them hate themselves for something that was completely out of their control. Recovery without deliverance is possible, but the feelings, consequences, or resulting behavior of that abuse will often remain. Deliverance gets rid of all of it because it casts out the demons that are inflicting the pain in the first place.

One of the first people I remember delivering was a 40-year-old lady who had been sexually abused by her father when she was a little girl. He would have her sit on his lap and proceed to grope her body parts. While he never had sexual intercourse with her, he would grope her on a regular basis; it also extended to a relative of hers. Neither girl spoke about it because of shame and, in a weird kind of way, to protect her father. For years she buried it, but all through her teenage years she suffered confusion about her sexuality and as a result hated the way she looked.

When she received deliverance, some of the demonic spirits that had entered her were fear, shame, guilt, abuse, sexual perversion, sadness, low self-esteem, lesbianism, and confusion. All these demons were able to gain entry or attachment initially through the spirit or demon of fear. The trauma of abuse by someone who should have been her protector caused her emotions of fear and guilt to overwhelm her.

When you have experienced abuse, whoever is the perpetrator, it alters the way you see yourself, what you believe you are worth, what you believe you deserve or don't deserve. It can even alter your sexuality. The confusion a spirit of abuse brings can completely change the trajectory of a person's life. It's that brain-altering condition called epigenetics where the phenotype (if you remember) is a genotype that has been altered because of environment, surroundings, or experience. Epigenetic traits are really common in people who have suffered abuse. Listen to this startling explanation of the damage it can cause in a young person:

Young brains are particularly sensitive to epigenetic changes. Experiences very early in life, when the brain is developing most rapidly, cause epigenetic adaptations that influence whether, when, and how genes release their instructions for building future capacity for health, skills, and resilience.[1]

When a young life has been traumatized, their personality and their God-given purpose has already started to change. In my experience, abuse is the most powerful change agent of the emotions in someone's life. It changes them from what they were purposed to be in their life to something dictated to by an unseen attack from the enemy. That lively child, the bubbly young girl, the person who was the life and soul of the party, the one who would never stop talking—it is all affected by the demonic spirit of abuse.

When it's sexual abuse that occurs at a young age, it can affect the person so much that they lose all sense of what is right and what is wrong as they grow up. They struggle to see themselves as God created them. As well as changing their personality, as I've already stated, it can also change and alter their sexual orientation. This is because sexual abuse is a perversion of what God originally created sex for. It's that knowing of what is right and what is wrong that gets clouded and confused. A sexually abused person just wants to feel secure and loved no matter where

that love or affirmation is coming from.

The good news in all of this is that even if you have suffered abuse of any kind, it doesn't have to be a permanent change—deliverance can set the captive free! The blood of Jesus, the word of God, and the casting out of demons can reverse any damage that has been caused through physical, sexual, or emotional abuse. It's only God who can make a person feel clean, pure, and brand new from the inside out!

Chapter 3
Entrance Through Abandonment and Rejection

This is one of the most interesting routes that can lead to demonic oppression. Not always, but most times people who have been abandoned when they were young—maybe left by their parents, given up for adoption, or not wanted in the womb—are directly harassed by demons. Demons can gain entrance primarily through rejection by a parent. However, rejec-

tion can also come from a spouse, a
partner, or even a schoolteacher, and
it is a spirit of rejection that will enter
a person. The door opens because of
what has been continually spoken
about the individual by someone who
has authority over them. The reason
this is interesting is because when the
feeling of being left, abandoned, or
rejected comes and the demon enters,
it also brings along with it a spirit of
rebellion and anger.

I remember delivering a young
girl of about ten years of age. Her
mother was at her wits' end with her.
She was unruly, angry, disobedient,
and would continually lie and make
up outrageous stories to gain attention
for herself and get people into trou-
ble. When we delved into her history,
we discovered that while the mom
was eight months pregnant with her,

the father beat the mom severely. Not only did he attack the mom, but he also repeatedly screamed that he didn't want the baby she was carrying and tried to kill the baby in her womb by strangling the mom. Thankfully, he was not successful, but the demons were able to gain entry because of the power of a parent's actions and words over their unborn child.

The spirit of rejection had gained access in the womb. Then, when she was born, it opened the door to many other spirits as she grew up. Spirits of rebellion, violence, aggression, lying, and the spirit of feeling unloved. The mom could not understand why the daughter displayed these traits as she was no longer with the father and, as much as she was able, showed love and kindness toward her daughter. The problem was that the demons had already gained entrance. When she was born, the child was already demonized. Her mother explained that she had always been a difficult child, and even as a baby she was continually agitated and would hardly ever settle. It was not surprising—those demons had already taken over the girl's personality, and being a young child, she had very little defense against such demons. Until we cast them out, the spirits of rejection and everything else that had entered were able to influence the soul of the daughter, causing bad behavior even from babyhood.

People who suffer with these types of demons from a very young age, because they have grown up with them, have very little awareness that this is the problem and will just assume, "This is the way I am." Sadly, parents who have no idea that this is the problem will take their children to the doctors and have them treated medically to try to cure, calm, or control the symptoms they are displaying.

There seems to be a diagnosis for every bad behavioral trait, and Satan loves that our children are being medicated at a faster speed than sound! Have you noticed the increase in diagnoses of ADHD, Asperger's syndrome, and autism over the last ten years?

Please hear me—I'm not saying that all children affected by these medical diagnoses or who have these symptoms have been demonized. But there are many for whom the root cause is not a deficit in their learning capacity, but it really is a demon. We can't imagine this is possible, especially that this could happen to an innocent baby, but that's when demons take their opportunity—at the most vulnerable time of our lives. Where is more vulnerable than when we are in our mother's womb?

I mentioned adoption and want to address this with as much sensitivity as possible. A spirit of rejection along with rebellion will always try and gain entrance to a baby or child who has been adopted. If you have adopted or fostered children, you may understand what I am saying. Maybe you have been adopted yourself, and as much as you have received love and care from the parents who raised you, there is still that emotion of rejection that rears its ugly head every now and again. The feeling of needing to be the best and impress those around you never goes away; the need to prove that you deserve what you have is endless, yet the underlying feelings of abandonment never quite go away. Anger is sometimes bubbling under the surface because of the situation you find yourself in, which was nothing to do with you.

I find it so interesting that people who have been adopted from the youngest age, even two weeks old, will still struggle with their identity and ultimately end up struggling with the feelings of rejection. We have prayed for many people in this situation. They will always say that they have so much love for the parents that raised them, but they still can't shake the deep-seated feeling of not being good enough. It's amazing to see, when that spirit of rejection is cast out of them, and the transformation begins to take place, they receive freedom and gain confidence in their identity because

of the overwhelming sense of Jesus' love for them. Praise God that the spirits of abandonment, rebellion, and anger must leave along with the spirit of rejection in the Name of Jesus!

Chapter 4
Entrance Through Pornography

Pornography is one of the biggest entry doors in the lives of humans. It may not always be through a bad experience that you encountered pornography; it could be because you have stumbled upon it at some point in your life. I will say, however, that most people who have been sexually abused or have had sexual experiences at a young age will have an addiction to pornography. The spirit of pornography will enter and take a hold of you if you become addicted to it, and all your willpower in the world will not be able to break you free from it.

The origins of this perversion originally started with Satan and his fallen angels perverting the beautiful gift of intimacy between a man and a woman. Nowhere more clearly can we see this than in Genesis 17 when we read the account of Sodom and Gomorrah and the sexual perversion that was taking place in that city. However, even further back in Genesis 6, we can read about the sons of God knowing or taking the daughters of men. The act of "knowing" one wife or one husband exclusively was a gift given from God to man. It meant forsaking all others for the purpose of creating new life on earth. Adam knew Eve, Abraham knew Sarah, and so on and so forth, but these heavenly beings stepped outside of their domain and had relations with human women. This was an abomination before God.

From the beginning we can see how Satan perverted sex. Sexual intercourse was created exclusively between a male and female, but both in Genesis 6 and 17 we find it had been perverted by the sons of God, the heavenly beings, with the daughters of men—human women who were willingly having sex with them, which produced the Nephilim, the race of giants. Its why God made the statement in Genesis 6:5-6 (NLT):

The Lord observed the extent of human wickedness on the earth, and he saw that everything they thought or imagined was consistently and totally evil. So the Lord was sorry he had ever made them and put them on the earth. It broke his heart.

Pornography became another distortion of God's creation of sex, and Satan realized he could snare billions of people with this kind of perversion.

Pornography is a huge lie. It takes what God has created, which is the act and enjoyment of sex between one man and one woman within the boundaries and security of marriage, and completely distorts its enjoyment and purpose. Instead of looking to your spouse to satisfy you—their body, their personality, their love for you—pornography leads us to believe that sex can be enjoyed just as much if not more as a selfish act on your own or with a stranger who doesn't require anything from you. The only demand that pornography has is self-gratification. Sex within marriage is all about loving and satisfying the other person and forsaking all others. Pornography is a selfish act all about satisfying self.

If Satan can blind us into thinking pornography is just another form of sex, then his plan to pollute our minds and hearts with perverted and distorted images of one another has no end. He can continually add definitions of what sex is while all along perverting the purity of what God originally created sex for. Today's distorted understanding of sex has produced a culture where any sexual act is becoming permissible.

Even though the world believes the lie that pornography is an alternative way of having sex, most believers have an overwhelming feeling of guilt once they have participated in it. Your conscience feels scarred, and your heart confirms that it's just not right. Yes, you read correctly—I said when *believers* participate in it! Studies show that over 50 percent of Christians, including pastors and leaders, admit to practicing pornography on a regular basis!

Demons gain entrance through pornography because it's sin. It's a hidden sin that no one else knows about. It's done in private, and once you have tried it, it can become addictive very quickly. Once you become addicted, demons enter. The thing with demons is they are perverted, unclean, and will twist everything.

Not everyone, but many people go from watching straight sex to homosexual sex to multiple people engaging in sex. For a minority of people, the demons twist things even further and they end up watching sex with young children and even sex with animals. This is one of Satan's greatest weapons against humanity. The demons involved are some of the worst, most twisted, dark, and devious demons we encounter. Pornography not only perverts our minds, but it also condemns our heart because we sin against ourselves. It's hidden, it causes anxiety, it brings confusion, it leaves a person unable to be satisfied with God's gift of intimacy and sex with their spouse, it distorts our view of the opposite sex, and it leaves us empty and void of satisfaction. It's the great deception that promises to make us feel complete yet does the exact opposite and, in fact, leaves us feeling dirty, guilty, and ashamed.

Because pornography is readily available to us 24/7, mainly via our mobile phones, it's one of the easiest sins to get addicted to and one of the most difficult to break free from. Most people have encountered pornography at some time in their life, and for those who encountered it when they were young, it seems an addiction to it is inevitable. I wouldn't be exaggerating if I said ninety percent of those we deliver have an issue with pornography, both men and women, with most starting at a young age. It may not even be the main reason they come for deliverance, but it seems to always be there somewhere in the background. It really is a difficult addiction to break, and even when people have been delivered from it, they must work hard at keeping free by not entertaining anything that could lead them back into it.

With any kind of deliverance, we will always encourage people to get rid of anything connected or associated with what they've been delivered from. With pornography, we encourage people to avoid watching or listening to anything with sexual content in it, especially when they are alone. We advise them not to spend ages in the bath or shower or even extended time in bed! I know this may sound extreme, but it works! You must replace those moments with spending time worshiping and praying. Deliverance gets rid of the demons, but it's the responsibility of the person to keep themselves free from any entering back in.

Chapter 5
Entrance Through Addiction

Addiction causes us to be out of control. We cannot control it; it controls us! In the book of Genesis, God specifically instructs man to have dominion and authority over the earth and everything that He has created in the earth.

Genesis 1:26 NKJV

Then God said, "Let Us make man in Our image, according to Our likeness; let them have dominion over the fish of the sea, over the birds of the air, and over the cattle, over all the earth and over every creeping thing that creeps on the earth."

According to the dictionary, *dominion* means "the power or right of governing and controlling, sovereign authority." We are meant to have power over everything on this earth. It's not something we attain to; it is something we have that was given to us originally by God, lost by Adam, but then regained by Jesus when He conquered all the powers of darkness on the cross. The dictionary definition of *addiction* is "a state of being compulsively committed to a habit or practice or to something that is psychologically or physically habit-forming, as drugs, to such an extent that its cessation causes severe trauma." Suddenly the substance, the alcohol, the porn, the drugs or whatever else we are addicted to has dominion over us, which is the opposite of how we should be living. It's a distortion of what God intended for man—that we should be in control and have dominion over things instead of things having dominion and control over us. Satan turns the tables in his favor.

Demons take advantage of this and once they are in, it is almost impossible to kick the addiction out through natural processes. Am I saying charities and organizations set up to help people overcome addictions don't work? Not at all; of course they work, *but* they cannot free someone completely of that addiction. Most ex-addicts work exceptionally hard to avoid "falling off the wagon" or going back into the addiction they have struggled with. If you've had any experience in this area, either as an ex-addict or someone helping an addict, you will know that the journey is relentless. It must be hard fought and without compromise.

It is one of the hardest roads to travel with a Christian because the very nature of addiction causes the person to be dependent on the addiction rather than on God. That is why they need deliverance, because it removes the problem at its root—the problem being the demons. It's almost irrelevant what the addiction is. It's the same wicked demon that has entered a person. It then allows the demons of the thing to which the person is addicted to enter, such as a spirit of pornography, obesity, alcohol, gambling, etc. Another reason the route of counseling or therapy to cure addictions can't work solely on its own is because a spiritual door has been opened and nothing in the natural world can overcome demons in the spiritual world. Determination, a strong self-will, goals, or classes cannot have dominion over the kingdom of darkness. It is only authority used in the Name of Jesus that demons respond to and are subject to.

Addictions can come in the form of alcohol, pornography, drugs, obesity, OCD, caffeine, gambling, and anything else that you cannot control in the natural. It goes beyond self-control and "trying" to be good. You can identify if you have a spirit of addiction in your life by not being able to live or function without the thing that you are addicted to. Just like the dictionary definition says, you have no control over it. When a spirit of addiction has entered, it must be cast out first before the spirits of the things you are addicted to can be broken and cast out. If this doesn't happen, the addiction will remain and all the feelings of needing the "fix" will come back later.

Before we were confident in operating fully in the ministry of deliverance, we would pray repeatedly for people struggling with all kinds of addictions. Demons would leave when they were cast out, but because we didn't cast out the strongman of addiction, it would allow all the ones we had cast out to come back again the moment the person had a weak moment. The individuals would be fine for a while, but then be drawn back into whatever they were addicted to. It was hard to watch because the feeling of failure would be overwhelming for both them and us. As we grew in this ministry, the Holy

Spirit revealed to us *how* we should cast this demon out and then how we should deal with the rest.

As I explain in later chapters, the ministry of deliverance is not just one quick prayer. Deliverance is a process. Time is taken to talk through a person's past, bringing to light buried and hidden things. Addictions of all kinds are always the result of some other trauma that has taken place in a person's life, and talking is the way we get to the root of it.

Chapter 6
Entrance Through Sin

Most demons have gained entrance to us before we are born again, but demons still have access to us as believers if we are in sin. If we continue to sin in areas we have been forgiven for, the door will remain open, so even though your spirit man is born again and you can have communion and fellowship with the Father, Son, and Holy Spirit, you are still choosing to allow Satan access to your soul man through continuing to sin. The Christian walk is one of dying to the flesh and walking in the spirit. Sin is making a conscious choice to walk in the flesh, and if we do this, we will never fulfill all that God has called us to do or ever be free of demonic influence or oppression. It never ceases to amaze me how many Christians still live like they are in the world. They have a relationship with the Lord, they are filled with the Holy Spirit, yet they still practice sin and think it's acceptable because they don't see any physical consequences.

I am truly not a "holier than thou" believer, but honestly some of the excuses Christians give for practicing sin are shocking! Let me just make things plain and clear and give you a list of the following sins that will allow demons to enter you as a Christian if you choose to practice sin: sex outside of marriage, addiction to pornography, masturbation, continually drinking alcohol and getting drunk, dishonesty, lying, abusive behavior toward people, always being angry at someone or something.

Sin could also take the form of unforgiveness or offense. The word of God is clear when it comes to unforgiveness. We are told in Matthew 6:14-15 (NKJV):

For if you forgive men their trespasses, your heavenly Father will also forgive you. But if you do not forgive men their trespasses, neither will your Father forgive your trespasses.

When we stand praying and asking God for anything, we must forgive our brother first; otherwise, God will not and cannot answer our prayers.

Mark 11:25-26 NKJV

And whenever you stand praying, if you have anything against anyone, forgive him, that your Father in heaven may also forgive you your trespasses. But if you do not forgive, neither will your Father in heaven forgive your trespasses.

When we become offended by a family member, a church leader, a brother or a sister in the church, or a work colleague, and we choose to live in offense, then demons will come in like a flood, and with one will come many! This sin is a favorite of theirs—they love to control believers within the church. In fact, that's where they can be most effective and cause the greatest damage. Demons love it when believers get offended and start to live with unforgiveness in their heart. Demons know what God's

word says and so they know that believers will struggle to get their
prayers answered if they don't forgive
as God has instructed them to. They
then influence believers and convince
them that God's word isn't completely true because He's not an-
swering their prayers! Again, I need
to say that neither Satan nor his
demons can stop us becoming born
again, but they can stop or delay us in
fulfilling God's call on our lives.

When demons are present in believers, poverty, failure, confusion,
instability, low self-esteem, apathy,
division, accusation, witchcraft, a religious spirit, to name just a few, will
show up in the church.

I know it's a lot to take in, especially as these entrances or open doors
I've described are just a few areas
where this can happen. Please be en-

couraged though, as you have read
this chapter and as you continue to
read through the book, just know the
enemy *is* defeated. Jesus said He
came to expose and destroy the works
of darkness, and our job is to carry out
His instructions in full.

1 John 3:8 NKJV

*For this purpose the Son of God
was manifested, that He might destroy
the works of the devil.*

Colossians 2:15 NKJV

*Having disarmed principalities
and powers, He made a public spec-
tacle of them, triumphing over them
in it.*

Chapter 7
Your Guide to Recognizing & Stopping Demonic Oppression

S o, let's get down to the "nitty gritty" of deliverance! What does it look like, how does it happen, and if I recognize that I have demons, how do I get rid of them?

I am going to take you through this as practically as I can, although there is a little more teaching here that's necessary for understanding. At the end, there will be a prayer to pray if you believe or recognize that you have demons. Freedom belongs to you because that's what Christ died and rose again for!

I want to reiterate at this point—demons gain their entrance in our lives through traumatic experiences, those experiences that produced fear, guilt, shame, or terror in us. This is just a small example of emotions.

In short, not everything is a demon! It's a natural part of human emotion to have negative thoughts and feelings. We live in a fallen world and there is so much to cause us concern. As believers we know we have overcome the world because Jesus said He has overcome the world and He lives on the inside of us, but we can still fall foul of all the negative stuff that surrounds us. Just because you have a sporadic emotion of anger, fear, guilt, anxiety, or stress does *not* mean you have a demon or that demons are on the inside of you. These types of emotions are natural to humans because of the fall, although as believers we can overcome them through the work of the Holy Spirit. It's important that I clarify this because I don't want any confusion about what being demonized looks like.

I just want to remind you again as a believer the areas you may be allowing Satan access into your life. Practicing sin as a Christian will open a door. So many Christians have one foot in the world and one foot in the church. Seriously, this is a dangerous place to be! You can cause more harm to yourself, your family, and your church by living this sort of life. Satan can manipulate you, influence you, and control you; he can also gain access to your finances. You become his puppet to destroy others who love the Lord. Sleeping around, getting drunk, watching pornography and practicing masturbation, purposely being dishonest, or knowingly walking in unforgiveness are all doors that will allow demons entry into your life. I'm not saying you don't love the Lord; you just may not fear Him if you are continually doing those things that He hates.

An area that most Christians are ignorant in is what you watch. Those things that you see or hear through your eye gate or ear gate and the negative atmospheres you surround yourself in will allow demons to enter, and if you allow this in your home, they will not just affect you but everyone living in your home. I heard an incredible message on "Atmospheres" by Pastor John Kilpatrick from the 1995 Brownsville Revival. He was explaining how lives were being radically changed during their nightly revival meetings, and specifically he was talking about marriages. Couples who hated one another beforehand, marriages that were on the brink of divorce, were being completely restored and delivered during the altar calls. The couples would often report that although during the services restoration would take place, the moment they arrived home, even pulling into the garage, their feelings of anger and frustration toward one another would return! They would then go back to the meetings, receive prayer, be restored once again, only to experience the same emotions when they returned home. There were so many stories like this that he went to prayer to ask the Holy Spirit what was happening.

Pastor John explained that they would regularly pray and clear the atmosphere in the sanctuary of any demons that they had cast out during altar calls and that they would invite the Holy Spirit to inhabit the place. He realized that this was the key! While in the revival, the atmosphere was full of faith, anointing, and God's presence because they had purposely invited Him to come and invade the space, but when these couples returned home, they were going back into the old atmosphere where arguments, anger, bitterness, and misunderstandings had reigned. He instructed every couple to cleanse the atmosphere in their home and to invite the Holy Spirit to reign in every room and in every area. When they did this, they reported that they had no more problems.

In the same message, Pastor John referred to how we invite demonic influences to enter our homes unchecked by what we allow to come through our television screens, our mobile phones, and our computers. He said our homes are like a platform in a railway station. The train comes along, the doors open, and whatever is on that train pours out into our home. The doors shut, the train leaves the station, but whatever got off that train stays in the home! An 18-rated movie, violence, adultery, lust, perversion, foul language. Our homes should be sanctuaries of peace where the Holy Spirit feels comfortable. They should not be comfortable dwellings for demons!

Another way we can become demonized is through any form of the occult, either practiced, watched, or entertained—it will always open a door! I believe most Christians recognize this and would not dream of practicing such things, but if you have ever been involved in the occult prior to being born again, then I would strongly encourage you that deliverance is needed, if you haven't already received it! I also wanted to mention it because the occult does not just involve Ouija boards, witches, divinations, spiritualists, or New Age! The dictionary definition says, "The occult is of or relating to magic, astrology, or any system claiming use or knowledge of secret or supernatural powers or agencies."

Doors are opened in our life when we are involved in anything outside of God that claims it has power to enhance our mind, body, or spirit. Meditation outside of God's word that encourages you to clear your mind or feel the energy on the inside of you is a form of the occult. Hypnosis where somebody else has access to control your mind for any period of time is a form of the occult. Practicing yoga, which has its roots in Hinduism and uses all the different positions of the "gods" to breathe and relax, is a form of the occult! Enneagram personality tests, reading predictions on social media like "Where will you be in five years' time?" all has its roots in fortune-telling, which is the occult!

How many of us click on those little games that pop up on our news feeds: "What does your name mean? Who will you marry? What does this year hold for you?" These things may sound harmless because in a way they are similar in nature to what we do as Christians. We meditate on His word by quietly praying and contemplating; we make vision boards, setting ourselves five-year goals! We must remember, however, that Satan takes God's truth and distorts it. He is able to deceive because he does it in a way that it is palatable even for the believer! So many Christians are involved in these kinds of practices, all of which originate in the occult.

I hope I haven't frightened you too much. Seriously, I have only mentioned a fraction of the occult practices many are unknowingly involved in! Sugar coating what really happens in the spiritual realm isn't going to help anyone! Revealing how and why demons gain access to us as Christians is! Truth and truth alone sets the captives free. We are affected by what happens in the spiritual realm a million times more than what happens in the natural realm.

So practically, what does the process of deliverance look like? Well, it is generally the same for all those who make an appointment to come to our office. We prepare a private space at the church so we will not be interrupted or overheard (we always lock the doors). We have tissues, water, and a sick bucket, and we make sure we are prayed up as ministers, as we dare not even attempt to do anything without the assurance of the anointing and the presence of God. It doesn't mean we spend hours in prayer before a deliverance, but it means we check in with the Holy Spirit to know and be assured of whose authority we are walking in and whose name we are using! We aim to have a team of at least three people. There will be one person who leads, and the others will support and speak in tongues quietly. We will always interact with one another. If one person hears from the Holy Spirit, we will allow that person to take the lead for a moment to call out the spirit, or they may just want to let the person leading know. Either way, the calling out of demons is done in an orderly fashion, calmly but forcibly and in unity.

There are five parts to a straightforward deliverance: counsel/talking, praying the prayer, breaking hereditary curses/bloodline ties, renouncing, and casting out. There are three things, however, that we require first from the person who is asking for deliverance. Number one, they must be honest—they cannot hide sins, hurts, or pain, past or present. We're bringing everything into the light. Satan is a legalist. He knows the word of God backward and forward, inside and out. If sins are hidden or you are too embarrassed to say what has happened to you, his demons are not going anywhere; they have a right to remain because the sin remains in the darkness.

Second, they cannot have unforgiveness in their heart toward anyone or anything. Satan knows the word and he knows if they won't forgive, he doesn't have to go anywhere, he can legally demonize them.

Matthew 6:14-15 NKJV
For if you forgive men their trespasses,
your heavenly Father will also forgive
you. But if you do not forgive men

*their trespasses, neither will your
Father forgive your trespasses.*

*Mark 11:25 NKJV
And whenever you stand praying, if
you have anything against anyone,
forgive him, that your Father in
heaven may also forgive you your
trespasses.*

*Luke 17:3-4 NKJV
Take heed to yourselves. If your
brother sins against you, rebuke him;
and if he repents, forgive him. And if
he sins against you seven times in a
day, and seven times in a day returns
to you, saying, "I repent," you shall
forgive him.*

Forgiveness may not always affect
the person who has hurt you, but it
will always affect you! When you for-

give, you release all power that Satan has over your life. You shut the door in his face, giving God access to bless you. Forgiveness also allows God to intervene in the situation, whereas unforgiveness ties His hands! If you don't let go but hold that person to account yourself, God cannot do anything. This is why it is vital that people forgive when receiving deliverance.

Third is the most necessary thing —they must be desperate! They cannot have an attitude of "I'll give it a go and see what happens" or think "If it doesn't work, I'll try something else." Just like the woman with the issue of blood, they must be all in and so desperate to get free that they don't care what they look like or who sees them!

As I have mentioned in a previous

chapter, I believe in counseling, and this is where it is used during deliverance. The first part is talking and investigating how doors were opened in the first place. Quite often within ten minutes we will identify many of the root causes, the hows and the whys. It is often a shock to the person, yet at the same time the penny drops for them and for the first time in their lives they realize why they have been struggling with certain issues for so long. Everything all at once makes sense! I cannot over emphasize the importance of this part of the deliverance ministry, and even before we move to the second part, people begin to receive their deliverance.

James 5:16 NKJV
Confess your trespasses to one another,
and pray for one another, that you may

*be healed. The effective, fervent prayer
of a righteous man avails much.*

This process is all about bringing to the light what has been hidden. Satan has power because he's the hidden evil behind all sickness and disease. When we expose him or his schemes, he loses his power to control, and it's almost as if the demons lose their grip to hold on to a person. I describe it as the truth being like oil—the demons have nothing to hook their claws into any longer. When you confess sin or sins that have been committed against you, deliverance and healing immediately begin.

Once we have established all of this and the person is able to bring to light all that they can remember, we will move on to the prayer, which is the second part of the deliverance.

The prayer covers several things that are necessary for deliverance. We use the same prayer that one of my favorite ministers on deliverance, Dr. Derek Prince, used. We ask the person to repeat the prayer audibly after one of us, line by line.

Lord Jesus Christ, I believe You died on the cross for my sins and rose again from the dead. You redeemed me by Your blood, and I belong to You, and I want to live for You.

I confess all my sins, known and unknown.

I'm sorry for them all; I renounce them all.

I forgive all others as I want You to forgive me.

Forgive me now and cleanse me with Your blood.

I thank You for the blood of Jesus

Christ, which cleanses me now from all sin.

And I come to You now as my deliverer.

You know my needs, every spirit that binds, that torments, that defiles.

That evil spirit, that unclean spirit.

I claim the promise of Your word: Whosoever that calls on the Name of the Lord shall be delivered.

I call upon You now.

In the Name of the Lord Jesus Christ, deliver me and set me free.

Satan, I renounce you and all your works.

I loose myself from you in the Name of Jesus, and I command you to leave me right now, in Jesus' Name.

Amen.

. . .

There are several important points this prayer covers—the first is salvation, making sure the person is born again. If they're not, then we take this opportunity for them to receive Jesus into their hearts. Second, they forgive all others. As we've already discussed, the demons are not going anywhere unless there is forgiveness. Sometimes they find it very difficult to say this part, but we labor on it if we must and make them say the names of the people they need to forgive. Many times, they will say it through gritted teeth or with tears streaming down their faces, but you *must* make sure they say this part. I will often encourage a person that even if they don't feel like it, everything we do as believers is by faith anyway, and this is just something else they are doing

by faith regardless of how they are feeling.

Third, they renounce the demons! This part is very powerful and even after the prayer we will get them to renounce emotions that have bound them (demonic spirits). The definition for the word *renounce* is "to repudiate; disown; to give up or put aside; to give up by formal declaration; to deny, disavow, discard, recant, cast off, divorce oneself from."

When the person being delivered renounces fear, guilt, shame, hatred, death, etc., we can then call those demons out because the person has vocally expressed that they no longer want them in their life or want to partner with them anymore! The demons must obey and leave.

After they have said the prayer, we

will instruct them to stand up and open their mouth slightly. Demons only come out one way, and that's through the mouth because they are spirit beings, like breath. Sometimes we will explain the manner of manifestation in which the demons will come out; other times we will just stay quiet. It's not a part of everyday normal life for most people, and so we never want to make them feel nervous about what is about to happen. We just allow the Holy Spirit to lead us through it all from beginning to end, even guiding what we say or what we don't say.

The third part is when we break every hereditary curse coming down from their ancestors or through their bloodline. This again is a very important part of deliverance, which I addressed in the early part of the book. (Chapter 1—read again if you have forgotten!) At this point we also break any unhealthy soul ties, whether they be sexual, emotional, or physical, again being led completely by the Holy Spirit.

The fourth part is where all the action generally happens, although many times at the point of breaking hereditary curses, the demons will start manifesting. We will have the person renounce all that they have spoken about, the things that have burdened them for years; it could be rejection, rebellion, addiction, hatred, idle words, abandonment, etc. Once they have done this, we will then make a statement like this:

Every demon attached to every-thing they have renounced, we command you to come out now in Jesus' Name, out now!

Immediately, demons will start to

manifest. Sometimes we will have to call them again and remind them that the person has renounced them and they can no longer stay. Demons hate to leave because it means they no longer have a body to use, which in turn means they cannot stay on the earth. They will try to hide, go quiet, or sometimes pretend they have gone! Through experience we are aware of all their tricks and know when they have really left.

There is always a mixture of manifestations. People may cough, retch, shout, contort, spin, crawl, jump, swing out, use expletive language, they may even burp demons out! Whatever way, I never cease to be amazed; demons are like petulant children who hate being told what to do. It's almost as if they stamp their feet and whine—they will cry and pretend to be the person to avoid being expelled, they will even hide in a body part and the person being delivered will suddenly get a pain in that area. This is how we know where they are—the person may say, "My head is pounding," "My back is aching," or, "I can't move my fingers." We will just command them to leave or sometimes we will touch that area and almost immediately they move and come out. Some deliverance ministers prefer not to touch those being delivered; for us we find this very effective when led by the Holy Spirit.

Demons will even make the person fall asleep by pretending they are free and are just resting. When they really don't want to go, they will try to argue their case, why they should stay. For me personally, I don't engage in much conversation with

demons. On occasion I will question the demon if the situation requires it, but demons are liars, so much of what they say is nonsense anyway. The normal verbiage from a demon is, "No, I won't leave," "She is mine," "I'm going to kill him." Sometimes they cackle and laugh in your face, mocking you. I will always close this stuff down straightaway and take control. If I am feeling particularly annoyed with the demon, I may tell it to shut up and get out. Normally, I will give instructions, especially when the demons won't allow the person to open their mouths. I will say something like, "Allow him to speak," or if they are rolling all over the floor and being particularly demonstrative, I will say, "Stop now and get up!" This may all sound a little strange, and at first it was weird interacting with

these evil spirits in this way, but when you recognize where they come from and the evil and misery they cause people, you understand why Jesus instructed us to do this. We are literally carrying out His command, which He has anointed us to do!

I will talk in the next chapter about what happens after someone has been delivered, but right now I want to give you instruction on self-deliverance. If you recognize that you personally need deliverance, you can do one of two things—you can make an appointment and ask a minister who is familiar with casting out demons to pray for you, or you can deal with it right now! I will say, having someone else pray for you initially is the best course of action (plus it reduces any probability that you have pride in your heart), but it is good to start the process off and deal with things the moment you recognize you have demons.

It's four simple steps.

The first step is to ask the Holy Spirit to reveal to you those doors that were opened in your life, giving access to the demons. Ask Him to give you discernment to know what demons they are. Once you have this information, then the second step is to pray the prayer. The third step is to renounce them. Remember, these are deep emotional struggles that you feel in the pit of your stomach, the emotions or addictions that continually harass you.

Renounce the demons, addressing them directly, and command them to go in Jesus' Name. Then, step four, you start to exhale and breathe them out. You may feel weird in your stomach or throat; you may start coughing or spitting up phlegm. Whatever happens, don't get freaked out! Demons go out in all manner of ways.

Let me give you this example so that you know you are doing it correctly. If the Holy Spirit has revealed to you that it is a spirit of self-hatred, insecurity, low self-esteem, then you would say something like this:

I renounce the spirit of self-hatred, of insecurity and low self-esteem, and in the Name of Jesus I command each one of you to leave me now! Out in Jesus' Name!

Then start to blow out.

You may need to repeat this process several times. You should have a lighter feeling on the inside of you as if a heavy weight has been lifted off your chest, shoulders, head,

or out of your stomach area. You should also be able to think a lot more clearly! Now take a moment to spend with the Holy Spirit, ask Him to fill you afresh, start to worship, and give God thanks for His goodness.

Recognize and Destroy Demonic Oppression

It's time to dive deeper and go on the offensive to destroy the strongholds of the enemy. Get Your Copy Today!

www.faithandflame.com/Devil_Come_Out

About Donna Howells

Donna Howells lives in South Wales, UK. Along with her husband Robbie, she pastors The Warehouse Church, as well as co-hosting their weekly tv program called Taking You Forward which airs on The Victory Channel and God TV. Donna is a gifted teacher with an ability to help people understand some of the weightier messages of the word.

www.ingramcontent.com/pod-product-compliance
Lightning Source LLC
Chambersburg PA
CBHW060131050426
42448CB00010B/2065